Grandparents
& Grandchildren

Grandparents
& Grandchildren

The delights of
being a grandparent

Camille Liscinsky

RYLAND

PETERS

& SMALL

LONDON NEW YORK

SENIOR DESIGNER Megan Smith
SENIOR EDITOR Clare Double
PICTURE RESEARCH Tracy Ogino
PRODUCTION Deborah Wehner
ART DIRECTOR Anne-Marie Bulat
EDITORIAL DIRECTOR Julia Charles
PUBLISHING DIRECTOR Alison Starling

First published in the
United States in 2006
by Ryland Peters & Small, Inc.
519 Broadway, 5th Floor
New York, NY 10012
www.rylandpeters.com

10 9 8 7 6 5 4 3 2 1

Text, design, and
commissioned photographs
© Ryland Peters & Small 2006
The following photographs are
© Stockbyte: 19, 21, 44–45, 54

ISBN-10: 1-84597-120-5
ISBN-13: 978-1-84597-120-5

Printed and bound in China

Contents

Introduction

Adults appear to transform when they become grandparents. It's as if they turn back the clock. Serious faces soften with silly grins. Rules about running in the house and jumping on the furniture are allowed to be broken. Five hundred miles is not too far to visit a newborn baby and the cookie jar is never, ever empty.

A Welsh proverb claims, "Perfect love sometimes does not come until the first grandchild." If such love involves wholehearted giving, the grandparents who contributed to this book would agree with the Welsh. It seems that the heart of a parent expands when a grandchild is born, welcoming a new generation to love. The grandparent takes on the role of a bridge between the past and the present. It's a role that feels wonderfully different and comfortably the same.

We give a hearty thank you to all the grandparents in this book who shared their reflections.

Wisdom

Be gentle with the young.

JUVENAL

It takes a lot of slow in order to grow.

Grandchildren get their learning
from parents and total acceptance
from grandparents.

*You've got to do your own
growing, no matter how
tall your grandparent was.*

IRISH PROVERB

Grandchildren want to tell you everything they're doing and for you to tell them that everything they're doing is just great!

When mothers and fathers say they're
sorry, children need to be big and brave
and forgive them.

Love each child as
an individual for
no two are alike.

A grandchild is a reminder to
bring a child's passion and
enthusiasm into your adult life.

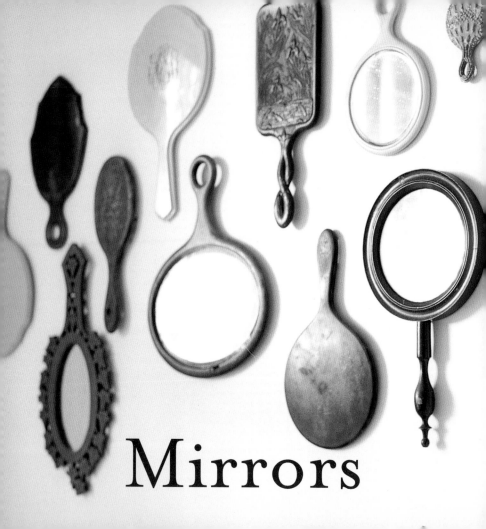

Mirrors

I am the family face.

THOMAS HARDY

Grandmothers are mothers with lots of frosting.

ANONYMOUS

As soon as I saw my
grandchild's face,
I fell in love.

When I look at my grandson,
I see my father's same sparkling
eyes, dotted with a brown fleck.
Grandchildren are a link to
our family's past and a bridge
to our family's future.

My granddaughter is so amazingly like me;
I actually see myself as a child when I look at
her. There I am, before my eyes, reincarnated.

I think of our four young grandchildren as embryonic personalities emerging from tiny newborn strangers.

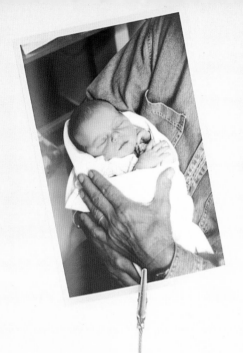

When our kids were young, they seemed so
vulnerable and needed so much looking after.
How could it be possible that they are raising kids
of their own? Where did they learn to do that?

23

Greatness of name in the father
oft times overwhelms the son;
They stand too near one another.
The shadow kills the growth: so
much, that we see the grandchild
come more and more oftener
to be the heir of the first.

BEN JONSON

If you know his father and grandfather, don't worry about his son.

AFRICAN PROVERB

Visits

Over the river and through the wood
To Grandfather's house we'll go.

Lydia M. Child

Being a grandmother can mean special treatment. My grandson was already two years old and hadn't begun to talk. One day he came to visit. As he bounded up the driveway he yelled his first words, "Granny Nanny, where are you? I'm here!"

When I visit my grandchildren,
I sing "Good Morning,
Sunshine" to the tune of
"You Are My Sunshine,"
and then make up lines to
match the weather of the day.
After a few mornings of this
nonsensical singing, I'm told,
"Grandma, if you don't know
the real words to the song,
I can teach you."

29

Being a granddad means
driving five hundred
miles in the snow to see
my first grandchild the
day he was born.

Living away from my
grandchildren means
creating special
connections. One
grandson and I play
imaginary games of
catch in the car, over
his brother's head,
and onto the train
as it pulls away.

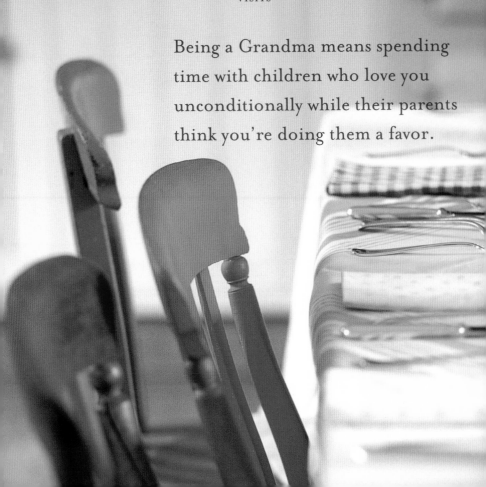

Being a Grandma means spending time with children who love you unconditionally while their parents think you're doing them a favor.

Coming to Grandma's house means shuffling through my cookie jar for favorite homemade cookies.

I'm amazed at the enormous patience I have as a grammy! I find myself clapping and cheering at our granddaughter with each jump she makes from the couch to the ottoman. Twenty-five years ago, I never would have encouraged such behavior!

33

Pride

*No cowboy was ever faster on the
draw than a grandparent pulling
a baby picture out of a wallet.*

ANONYMOUS

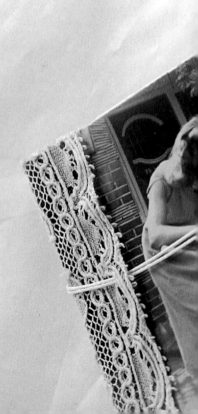

When I visited my grandson's
class as a guest speaker, I
caught a glimpse of him
beaming, proud as can be.
How short is this period of
time when a grandchild does
not distance himself from the
older generation?

Being a grandfather allowed me to
experience my grandson's victory the day
he got off the ski lift without falling.

I'm the one my grandson turns to
when our family gathers and there's
lots of noise and clatter.
He leans closely and says,
"Grandma, read
me a story in
a whisper."

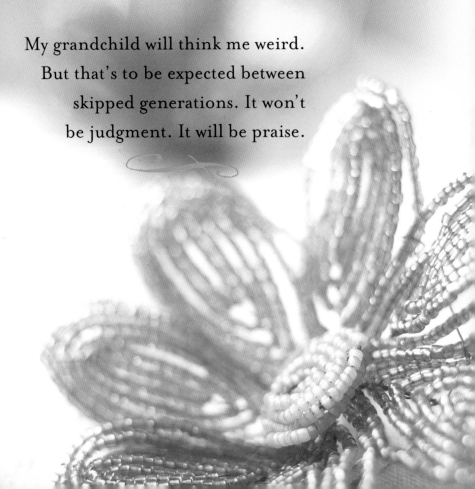

My grandchild will think me weird.
But that's to be expected between
skipped generations. It won't
be judgment. It will be praise.

One of life's mysteries is how the boy who wasn't good enough to marry your daughter can be the father of the smartest grandchild in the world.

JEWISH PROVERB

My home has a well-stocked bar, but the most important bottles are four small, empty ones. When each grandchild was born I asked the nurse for the first bottle they drank from. To me, the bottles had contained the world's finest brew.

Being a grandparent is like starting
life all over again. There are a lot of
grandparents in this world who hold
generations of children in their hearts
and I, happily, am one of them.

*Man is the only creature on earth
that has come to have knowledge of
his grandparents and grandchildren.*

BAAL SHEM TOV

Delights

A grandparent is a little bit teacher,

a little bit parent, and a little bit best friend.

ANONYMOUS

Being a grandparent means reliving happy moments I spent with my children—the first day of school, the loss of a tooth, homemade valentines—and the anxious moments, too, like having a sick child or spending the night in the hospital.

There are fathers who do not love their children; there is no grandfather who does not adore his grandchild.

VICTOR HUGO

Kids see grandparents as avenues of pure love.

My husband and I are grateful that our grandchildren's existence guarantees us a continuing stake in the future, but we are deeply relieved that most of the responsibility rests on their parents' shoulders.

I'm 83, have arthritis and gray hair, but being a grandmother makes me feel young.

*It is such a grand thing to be the
mother of a mother; that's why
the world calls her grandmother.*

ANONYMOUS

The first time my granddaughter called me
Grandma I became a special person in her life.

When my grandson grasped my
finger, he lassoed my heart.

A grandparent's heart is big enough to hold a grandchild's secrets.

A New Role

Perfect love sometimes does not come until the first grandchild.

WELSH PROVERB

A grandfather's great big hands are
the softest cradle a baby can have.

If nothing is good, well,
call your grandmother.

ITALIAN PROVERB

How does a tiny, seven-pound
newborn bring her strapping
6'2" grandfather to tears
when he has to leave her and
catch a plane back home?

Being a grandparent is the best "do over" there is—
a chance to put into action with the next generation
all those "if I had to do it over again" resolutions.

Grandparents are the eyes at
the back of a parent's head.

I so enjoy the pride I see in
my children's eyes and hear
in their voices when they
talk about their children—
our grandchildren.

My role as a grandfather is a balancing
act between indulging and disciplining,
instructing and comforting.

Being a grandparent means being close to two
generations before me and two generations after me.
It's remembering those before me who shaped my
life and wanting to be remembered by those after
me, whose lives I hope I have influenced.

*Children's children are
the crown of the aged.*

PROVERBS 17:6

Acknowledgments

a=above, b=below, l=left, r=right, c=center

The author and publisher would like to thank
the contributors who made this book possible:

Anonymous, pages 51, 54; Joan Bachand, page 29; Carolyn Batchelor, pages 22, 48; Frank Batchelor, page 60 a; Sylvia Breakey, page 30 r; Denny Clapp, page 14 b; Meg Clapp, page 33 b; Betty Dirstine, page 14 a; Ken Forbes, page 47; Adela Franco, page 46 a; David Hockman, page 36 b; Jean Hockman, page 58 b; Phyllis James, pages 19, 50 c; Peggy Marrin Johnson, page 39; Loretta Kujawa, pages 42, 49; Agnes Liscinsky, page 33 a; Mary Lubeley, pages 13, 32, 57 b; Kay Marciniak, pages 50 b, 57 a; Tom Marciniak, page 60 b; Chris Owenson, page 10 a; Walter Raczkowski, pages 30 l, 41; Peggy Reid, page 37; Mary Schroer, page 21 b; Nancy Smith, page 21 a; Nancy Stepanovich, page 28; Carole Watkins, page 58 a; Rick Whelan, pages 23, 36 a; Helen Whitaker, pages 10 b, 12.

Picture credits

ph=photographer, a=above, b=below

ph Caroline Arber: 6 inset, 34–35

ph Jan Baldwin: 24

ph Vanessa Davies: 33

ph Christopher Drake: 29 a Vivien Lawrence, an interior
designer in London (+44 20 8209 0562),
29 b Clara Baille's house on the Isle of Wight

ph Dan Duchars: 18, 42, 61

ph Melanie Eclare: 10–11

ph Emma Lee: 60

ph Tom Leighton: 31 the Amsterdam loft of
Aleid Röntgen-Brederode and her sister Annette Brederode,
antique collectors "Les Brocanteuses," 55

ph James Merrell: 38

ph Debi Treloar: 3, 8–9, 12–13, 15–17, 20, 23, 28, 30, 32, 37 Sophie Eadie's house in London, 40–41, 43, 59

ph Chris Tubbs: 25–27, 57 background

ph Jo Tyler: 6 background

ph Alan Williams: 52–53 the Norfolk home of Geoff and Gilly Newberry of Bennison Fabrics (www.bennisonfabrics.com)

ph Polly Wreford: endpapers, 1–2, 4–5, 22, 39, 46–47, 48 featured photographs by Julia Bostock, 49–50 background, 51, 56

© Stockbyte: 19, 21, 44–45, 54